YOUR KNOWLEDGE HAS VALUE

- We will publish your bachelor's and master's thesis, essays and papers

- Your own eBook and book - sold worldwide in all relevant shops

- Earn money with each sale

Upload your text at www.GRIN.com and publish for free

Performance Analysis of Searching Algorithms

Mohamed Eshtawie
Waafa Alrahman
Nuri Elshamam

Bibliographic information published by the German National Library:

The German National Library lists this publication in the National Bibliography; detailed bibliographic data are available on the Internet at http://dnb.dnb.de.

ISBN: 9783346511256
This book is also available as an ebook.

© GRIN Publishing GmbH
Nymphenburger Straße 86
80636 München

All rights reserved

Print and binding: Books on Demand GmbH, Norderstedt, Germany
Printed on acid-free paper from responsible sources.

The present work has been carefully prepared. Nevertheless, authors and publishers do not incur liability for the correctness of information, notes, links and advice as well as any printing errors.

GRIN web shop: https://www.grin.com/document/1134609

Performance Analysis of Searching Algorithms for Solving NP-Complete in AI Problems

Mohamed almahdi Eshtawie
Wafaa Abdallah Abed Alrahman
Nuri Abrahem Elshamam
Dep. of Information Technology
Asmarya Islamic University

Abstract – **Problem solving is an essential topic in Artificial Intelligence study and application. It is concerned with solving mathematical problems and clues such as puzzles.** The study is **primarily concerned** with the ability of some searching algorithms such as Restricted Boltzmann Machines, Message Passing, Breadth First Search and Depth First Search to Solve Sudoku puzzle problems in the area of AI. For each of these methods, a code in Java language will be written and executed so that performance analysis can take place. A comparison analysis between the selected algorithms will be done. The analysis will cover some parameters e.g. **Time, space, optimality, completeness.**

keywords—**tree graph, Sudoku puzzles, problem solving, time complexity, completeness.**

I. INTRODUCTION

Problem solving in AI may be characterize as a systematic search through a range of possible actions in order to reach some predefined goal or solution. The real art of problem solving is in deciding the description of the states and operators. With this regard, there are different kinds of searching algorithms applied in artificial intelligence used for problem solving. There is a variety of problems in artificial intelligence area many of which are mathematical based in nature. Sudoku puzzle is a mathematical based problem considered as one of major problems addressed by researcher for solving. In late of 1990s, Sudoku is one of the interesting problems that gained popularity. It is not considered as a confusing and complex and therefore, may be dealt with by pencil and eraser. Many of the researchers started looking for tools, steps or methods to solve Sudoku using computer applying uninformed searching algorithms. The problem needs to be solved is formulated through the state space based on the nature of tools applied. During this process, search tree is generated by taking initial state and applying the successive function to it. The way problems are described can be formulated as follows:

1. *Initial State*: the initial state describes the situation at which problem starts.
2. *Successor function*: an intermediate states or functions describe the possible actions and their outcomes.
3. *Goal Test:* determines if the given state is the goal state or not. For example; in chess the goal is to reach a state called checkmate where the opponent's king is under attack and can't escape.
4. *Path Cost*: A path cost is a function that assigns a numeric cost to each path. The problem-solving agents choose a cost that reflects its own performance measure, e.g. path distance between the cities, (Russell & Norvig, 2010).

Sudoku puzzles problem:

Sudoku is a popular logic-based combinatorial puzzle game {1, 2, 3...9}. It is consisting of 81 cells, contained in a 9x9 grid (Behrooz, 2009). Each cell can contain a single integer ranging between one and nine as shown in Fig 1.

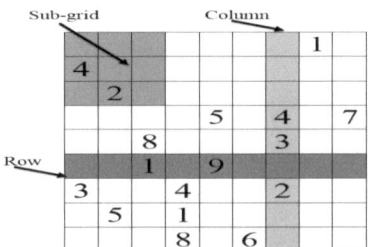

Figure 1. 9x9 Sudoku Puzzle grids

✓ Each row of cells is only allowed to contain the integers one through nine exactly once.
✓ Each column of cells is only allowed to contain the integers one through nine exactly once.
✓ Each 3x3 sub-grid is also allowed only to contain the integers one through nine exactly once.

II. SEARCHING ALGORITHMS

Problem solving is basically a search or tracing towards the goal or solution of the puzzle. However there are many searching algorithms among which four have been applied in this paper. Following is a brief description of the used algorithms:

1. *Restricted Boltzmann Machine algorithm (RBM):* Boltzmann machines is a class of neural networks introduced in late 1980's. They are based on statistical physics. In contrary to most other neural network methods, Boltzmann Machines are probabilistic graphical models that can be interpreted as stochastic neurons (Wolfgang Maass, 2014). Boltzmann machines where connections between the hidden neurons and the visible neurons in the original Boltzmann, RBM is an energy based model and the energy between visible and hidden units as in (Ruslan, et al., 2007).

$$E(v,h,\theta) = -\sum_{i=1}^{D}\sum_{j=1}^{F}W_{ij}v_{i}h_{j} - \sum_{i=1}^{D}b_{i}v_{j} - \sum_{j=1}^{F}a_{j}h_{j} \quad (1)$$

Where $\theta = \{W,a,b\}$ represent the parameters of the model. W_{ij} represents the symmetric weight between i^{th} visible unit and the jth hidden. The connection between bias term and the ith visible unit is defined by b_i. a_j connection between bias unit and the jth hidden unit. v and h represent the visible and hidden vectors respectively. Weights are stored in a weight matrix as in (2).

$$W_{ii} = \begin{cases} 0 & v_i \\ w_{ji} & v_{i,j} \end{cases} \quad (2)$$

The other properties of unique rows, unique columns and unique sub-grid are encoded in the same way but processed with the whole weight matrix. Equation 3 presents the joint probability distribution of visible and hidden units (Navdeep & Geoffrey, 2011).

$$p(v,h,\theta) = \frac{1}{Z(\theta)} e^{-E(v,h,\theta)} \quad (3)$$

$$Z(\theta) = \sum_{v}\sum_{h} e^{-E(v,h,\theta)} \quad (4)$$

Due to stochastic nature of Boltzmann machines there is a separate probability function used to determine if a single neuron should flip its state during a discrete time step. The probability that the model assigns to the visible vector v as in (5).

$$p(v,\theta) = \frac{1}{Z(\theta)} \sum_{h} e^{-E(v,h,\theta)} \quad (5)$$

2. *Message Passing algorithm (MP):* Message passing provides powerful approximation algorithms for problems that can be formulated in terms of, probabilistic, graphical models such as factor graphs that used to represent factorization of a probability distribution function. (Arunkumar & Komala, 2015). Enabling efficient computations, such as the computation of marginal distributions through the sum-product algorithm in loopy graphical models (Frank R, et.al, 2001; Jonathan S, et.al, 2005). The sum-product algorithm in loopy graphical models, normally presented as message update equations on a factor graph, involving messages between variable nodes and their neighboring factor nodes and vice versa is based on passing messages between adjacent nodes of the underlying factor graph (Andre, et al., 2014; Frank R, et al., 2001). The following is the sum-product equations.

The constraint-to-variable messages as in (6).

$$r_{mn}(x) = \sum_{\{n' \in N_{m,n}\} \atop n=x, n'=x_{n}, allunique} \prod_{l \in N_{m,n}} q_{lm}(x_l) \qquad (6)$$

Where is $n=x$ the variable node in vector $N_{m,n}$ and $n'=x_n$ represent the neighbours of x in Factor Graph (FG) that all are unique. The Posteriori beliefs is presented as in (7) (Kristian, et al., 2009).

$$q_n(x) = P(n = x) \prod_{m \in M_n} r_{mn}(x) \qquad (7)$$

The message m is a vector must contain all possibility of factor node into the specific domain M_n for a variable node. The variable-to-constraint messages as in (8).

$$q_{n,m}(x) = P(n = x) \prod_{m' M_{n,m}} r_{mn}(x) \qquad (8)$$

Represent $P(n=x)$ a priori probabilities vector, if the variable node is k then the element k in probability vector is 1 and all other elements are 0. And $m' \in M_{n,m}$ represent the neighbours of a message m into the specific domain $M_{n,m}$ (Olusegun, et al., 2014).

3. *Breadth First Search algorithm (BFS):* Is an algorithm for traversing or searching a tree, tree structure, or graph. One starts at the root, selecting a node as a root(Rong & Eric A, 2006). This root node will be at the top of the tree. The top is searched and it is level-by-level traversal and then the nodes below are searched for the solution . The properties of BFS are presented in Table 1. It exhaustively searches the entire graph or sequence without considering the goal node or solution until it finds it. From the standpoint of the algorithm, all child nodes obtained by expanding a node are added to a First in_First out queue. First in_First out mean that nodes accessed first explored or expanded first. This elaborates the level-by-level traversal policy.

TABLE 1. THE PROPERTIES OF BREADTH FIRST SEARCH

Property	Description
Class	Search algorithms
Data structure	Graph
Worst case performance	$O(|V|+|E|) = O(b^d)$ every vertex and every edge will be explored in the worst case. $|V|$ is the number of vertices and $|E|$ s the number of edges in the graph.
Worst case space complexity	$O(|V|) = O(b^d)$ to find the nodes that are at distance d from the start node (measured in number of edge traversals) where b is the "branching factor" of the graph.

4. *Depth First Search algorithm (DFS)*: As a searching algorithm, DFS is applied for traversing graph or a tree structure. One starts at the root (selecting a node as the root in the graph case) and explores as far as possible along each branch before backtracking (Farhad, et al., 2012). Backtracking mean traversing to the upper level since the present position is not the goal state or solution. As searching DFS is typically used to traverse an entire graph, and takes time $O(|V| + |E|)$, linear in the size of the graph. In these applications it also uses space $O(|V|)$ in the worst case to store the stack of vertices on the current search path as well as the set of already-visited vertices as in Table 2.

TABLE 2. THE PROPERTIES OF DEPTH FIRST SEARCH

Property	Description
Class	Search algorithms
Data structure	Graph
Worst case performance	$O(|V| + |E|)$ for explicit graphs traversed without repetition, $O(b^d)$ for implicit graphs with branching, factor b searched to depth d
Worst case space complexity	$O(|V|)$ if entire graph is traversed without repetition, O(longest path length searched) for implicit graphs without elimination of duplicate nodes

III. CONSTRAINT SATISFACTION PROBLEMS

The Sudoku puzzle is a special case of a more general type of problems called constraint satisfaction problems. Constraint satisfaction problem is a collection of variables all of which have to be assigned values that are subject to specified constraints. Computational problems like scheduling a collection of tasks, or interpreting a visual image, can all be seen as CSPs. We are interested in finding a satisfying assignment for the CSPs, which means that we need to assign values to each of the variables from their respective domain spaces (Todd K & Jacob H, 2006), such that all the constraints are satisfied. Figure 2. Show Sudoku with Constraint Satisfaction.

```
        C10 C11 C12  C13 C14 C15  C16 C17 C18
   C1   ⎛ 1   2   3⎞⎛ 4   5   6⎞⎛ 7   8   9⎞
   C2   ⎜10  11  12⎟⎜13  14  15⎟⎜16  17  18⎟
   C3   ⎝19  20  21⎠⎝22  23  24⎠⎝25  26  27⎠
   C4   ⎛28  29  30⎞⎛31  32  33⎞⎛34  35  36⎞
   C5   ⎜37  38  39⎟⎜40  41  42⎟⎜43  44  45⎟
   C6   ⎝46  47  48⎠⎝49  50  51⎠⎝52  53  54⎠
   C7   ⎛55  56  57⎞⎛58  59  60⎞⎛61  62  63⎞
   C8   ⎜64  65  66⎟⎜67  68  69⎟⎜70  71  72⎟
   C9   ⎝73  74  75⎠⎝76  77  78⎠⎝79  80  81⎠
```

Figure 2. Sudoku with Constraint Satisfaction

Constraint Satisfaction Problem can be defined as the 9×9 Sudoku puzzles define constraints as:

- ✓ Variables: empty slots
- ✓ Domains = {1,2,3,4,5,6,7,8,9}
- ✓ Constraints: 27 all-different

IV. SUDOKU PROBLEM SOLVING

A. Restricted Boltzmann Machine Solver

For implementing RBM, the energy measure with weights and the state associated for every node of the 81×9 =729 nodes in Sudoku network. This is used to determine if the state of single neuron should be flipped is defined. Each node has a binary state of either on or off. This is also translated to solutions, where only one of every nine neurons in groups will be in the state on. For every number being placed on the grid, there is nine possible assignments, and the probability of a neuron being active as in (9).

$$p_{i=on} = \frac{1}{1 + e^{-\Delta E/T}} \qquad (9)$$

E is the summed-up energy of the whole network into neuron i, which is a fully connected to all other neurons. T is a temperature constant controlling the rate of change during several evaluations with the probability $p_{i=on}$ during simulation. A neuron "i" as in Fig 3.

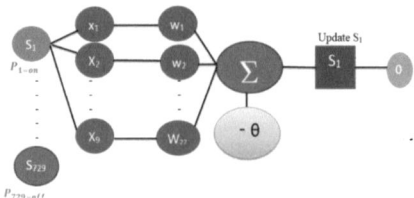

Figure 3. A single neuron in Sudoku grid

Message Passing Solver

The Sudoku puzzle can be represented as a bipartite graph. In the graph, 9x9 Sudoku puzzle cells can be mapped to set 'S' and all the constraints that need to be satisfied can be mapped to set 'C'. All cells (S_n) are mapped to the set 'S' by sending probabilistic messages between adjacent nodes. Each message m is a vector, must contain all possible numbers as Domain= {1, 2, 3, 4, 5, 6, 7, 8, 9}, meaning the possibility of one number can be filled into the specific cell. After several rounds of message passing, the different row, column and sub-grid constraints (C_m) are mapped to a set 'C' in that order. Once the two sets are defined, edges are introduced based on the relationship between the cell and the constraint. An (undirected) edge is presented between a cell node and a constraint node, if the constraint is applicable to that cell node.

Sudoku with constraints satisfaction shown in Fig 2. is mapped applying message passing as presented in Fig 4 show that the numbers of cell nodes is 81 and the numbers of constraint nodes in 27. The domain associated with each cell node is 9. Dimensions of N_m matrix is 27×9=243. Dimensions of M_n matrix is 81×3=243.

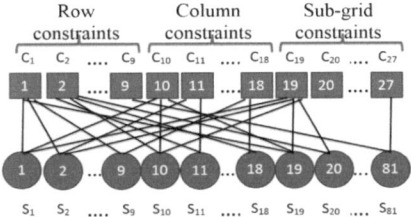

Figure 4. The factor graph of a 9 × 9 Sudoku solver

B. Breadth First Search Solver

BFS is a general technique of traversing a graph. A path-finding algorithm is capable of always finding the solution, if one exists. BFS expands nodes in order of their distance from the root level-by-level; each node in the search tree is expanded in a breadth wise at each level. These all expanded nodes are retained till the search is completed (Scott, et al., 2012).

The concept of a queue to expand the states from a graph is used. The Breadth-First Search expands the nodes horizontally and the expansion process storing one copy of the board for each state. As in Fig 5. (a) and (b) Copy of the board.

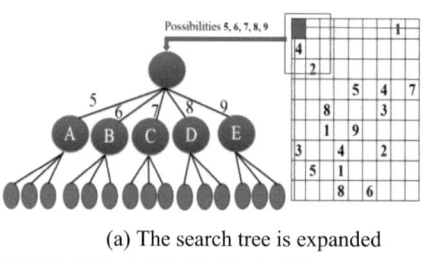

(a) The search tree is expanded

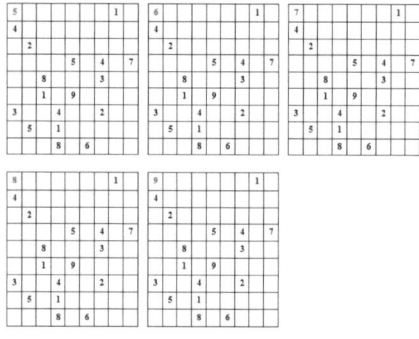

(b) Copy of the board

Figure 5. First step searching using Breadth-First Search

As in Fig 5. A and E were already expanded, these they do not belong to the queue anymore. The expansion order is

inverse to the creation order. This the five first nodes were generated in the order as follows: 1st - A, 2nd - B, 3rd - C, 4th - D and 5th - E. The first node to be expanded is the first node inserted in the queue - node A.

C. Depth First Search Solver

This algorithm choose to go deeper in the tree or graph. DFS visits all the vertices in the graph using the concept of a stack to expand nodes vertically and after DFS visited all the reachable vertices from particular source vertices. It chooses one of the remaining undiscovered vertices and continue the search. In addition, stop increasing the depth only if a goal or a dead-end is reached. To make this mechanism possible, the algorithm uses the concept of a Last_ in First_out LIFO Queue as in Fig 5. (a) and (b) Copy of the board.

Similar to FIFO, the expansion order is inverse as the created order. This the five first nodes were generated in the order as follows: 1st - A, 2nd - B, 3rd - C, $4t^{h}$ – D, and 5th - E. and storing one copy of the board for each state. The first node to be expanded is the last node inserted in the queue E.

V. EVALUATING PROBLEM-SOLVING PERFORMANCE:

It is known that when applying different tools to deal with or to solve the same problem, there are some factors that need to be taken into account in order to evaluate the performance of these different tools. Time, space, optimality, and completeness are the four main parameters that can lead to real evaluation when applying different tools to the same problem.

Time Complexity: defined as the maximum time taken to solve the Sudoku puzzle. This parameter differs from one algorithm to another as follows:

For Boltzmann machine the time complexity is N^3, since it is checking a row then a column and then a block hence takes $N*N*N$ as a total time to check. And solving time is 0.008257536 seconds.

In the case of message passing checking is by the puzzle itself. Therefore, the time is so long and cannot be controlled by the algorithm. Its way of checking will be row, column, block, and grid. This means that the time is $N*N*N*N$ or N^4. And solving time is 8.3777421E10 seconds.

The Breadth first search complexity time is $O(b^d)$ where b is branches length generated by Sudoku and d is the depth of that branch. There are 9^{81} attempts. And solving time is 81.58229 seconds.

Depth first search $O(b^m)$. In this case b is 9 and m equals 81, there are 9 attempts. And solving time is 36.67437 seconds.

Space Complexity: Similar to the time complexity, but it represents the maximum space required for Sudoku to be solved. For the different algorithms applied, these four parameters are as follows. In Boltzmann, $O(DN^3)$, where d is depth of network structure and N^3 is the maximum time to find a solution for the reduced 3x3 grid. Massage passing: the space complexity is calculated based on the probability where V represents the vector. In the case BFS, the space complexity is $O(b^d)$ when having regular 9 x 9 Sudoku. Here b equals 9 and m equals 81, hence there are 9^{81} nodes open at the deepest level. The space complexity in DFS, $O(bm)$, where b is branching factor of tree structure and m is maximum depth of answer in tree structure. $O(b \times m)$ there will only be $9 \times 81 = 729$ nodes open at a time.

Optimality: the optimality refers to an optimal way to find a solution. In some cases a solution can be found but not with an optimal path or way. This affects to a great extend the time taken for the solution and the memory and other parameters used. When referring to the different algorithms we found that the Boltzmann can be considered as an optimum among the four applied from the execution time point of view and it has different solution for the same Sudoku as well. On the other hand, the Depth First search is an optimal from solutions point of view but with time longer than that of Boltzmann algorithm. The following presents this result.

	0 0 0 0 0 0 0 1 0
	4 0 0 0 0 0 0 0 0
	0 2 0 0 0 0 0 0 0
	0 0 0 0 5 0 4 0 7
	0 0 8 0 0 0 3 0 0
	0 0 1 0 9 0 0 0 0
	3 0 0 4 0 0 2 0 0
	0 5 0 1 0 0 0 0 0
	0 0 0 8 0 6 0 0 0
	(a) Sudoku problem
8 9 5 7 6 3 2 1 4	6 9 3 7 8 4 5 1 2
4 3 6 9 1 2 8 7 5	4 8 7 5 1 2 9 3 6
1 2 7 5 8 4 6 3 9	1 2 5 9 6 3 8 7 4
9 6 3 2 5 8 4 1 7	9 3 2 6 5 1 4 8 7
5 7 8 6 4 1 3 9 2	5 6 8 2 4 7 3 9 1
2 4 1 3 9 7 5 8 6	7 4 1 3 9 8 6 2 5
3 8 9 4 7 5 2 6 1	3 1 9 4 7 5 2 6 8
6 5 2 1 3 9 7 4 8	8 5 6 1 2 9 7 4 3
7 1 4 8 2 6 9 5 3	2 7 4 8 3 6 1 5 9
(b) Boltzmann solution	(c) Message passing solution
6 9 3 7 8 4 5 1 2	6 9 3 7 8 4 5 1 2
4 8 7 5 1 2 9 3 6	4 8 7 5 1 2 9 3 6
1 2 5 9 6 3 8 7 4	1 2 5 9 6 3 8 7 4
9 3 2 6 5 1 4 8 7	9 3 2 6 5 1 4 8 7
5 6 8 2 4 7 3 9 1	5 6 8 2 4 7 3 9 1
7 4 1 3 9 8 6 2 5	7 4 1 3 9 8 6 2 5
3 1 9 4 7 5 2 6 8	3 1 9 4 7 5 2 6 8
8 5 6 1 2 9 7 4 3	8 5 6 1 2 9 7 4 3
2 7 4 8 3 6 1 5 9	2 7 4 8 3 6 1 5 9
(d) Breadth first search solution	(e) Depth first search solution

Figure 6. A sample of 17 clues Sudoku puzzles with four results

Completeness: if the algorithm was able to find all solutions for the Sudoku regardless the execution time, then it is said to be complete. This study shows the Boltzmann machine and Depth first algorithm is complete since that able to solve Sudoku puzzles with sort execution time.

TABLE 3. ALGORITHMS PERFORMANCE FOR SOLVING PROBLEM

Algorithm	Time Complexity	Space Complexity	Optimality	Completeness
Restricted Boltzmann Machine	$O(N^3)$	$O(DN^3)$	Yes	yes
Message passing	$O(N^4)$	$O(\|V\| \exp(\max xV \in V \|L(V)\|))$	No	No
Breadth First Search	$O(b^d)$	$O(b^d)$	No	No
Depth First Search	$O(b^m)$	$O(bm)$	Yes	Yes

VI. CONCLUSION

The study is primarily concerned with Searching Algorithms i.e. Breadth First Search and Depth First Search for Problem Solving mechanisms in the field of artificial intelligence. In addition, Restricted Boltzmann Machine as a kind of neural network and Message passing Algorithm have been studied and applied for problem solving. In order to determine their ability for problem solving so that their performance, significance, and hence a comparison between them is made, 9×9 Sudoku puzzles is used as a case study in this research. The results show that the Restricted Boltzmann Machine algorithm is the best among all four algorithms covered in this study.

VII. REFERENCES

[1] Russell, S., & Norvig, P. (2010). Chapters 3 and 4. In *Artificial Intelligence: A Modern Approach* (Vol. 3rd Edition).

[2] Behrooz, P. (2009). Motivating Computer Engineering Freshmen Through Mathematical and Logical Puzzles. *TRANSACTIONS ON EDUCATION. VOL. 52, NO. 3.* IEEE.

[3] Wolfgang Maass. (2014, May). Noise as a Resource for Computation and Learning in Networks of Spiking Neurons. *Proceedings of the IEEE, 102*(5), pp. 861-880.

[4] Arunkumar, B., & Komala, R. (2015, July 7). Applications of Bipartite Graph in diverse fields including cloud computing. *International Journal Of Modern Engineering Research (IJMER)*(5).

[5] Frank R, K., Brendan J, F., & Hans-An. (2001). Factor graphs and the sum-product algorithm. *IEEE Transactions on Information Theory, 47(2), 498–519.*

[6] Jonathan S, Y., William T, F., & YairWeiss. (2005, July). Constructing free energy approximations and generalized belief propagation algorithms. *IEEE Transactions on Information Theory, 51(7).*

[7] Rong, Z., & Eric, A. (2009). Combining Breadth-First and Depth-First Strategies in Searching for Treewidth. *The twenty-First International Joint AAAI Conferece on Artifical Intelligence*, (pp. 641-645).

[8] Farhad, S., Bahareh, S., & Golriz, F. (2012, September). A New Solution for N-Queens Problem using Blind Approaches: DFS and BFS Algorithms. *International Journal of Computer Applications (0975 – 8887), Volume 53– No.1.*

[9] Ruslan, S., Andriy, M., & Geoffrey E., H. (2007). Restricted Boltzmann machines or collaborative filtering. *In Proceedings of the 24th international conference on Machine learning* (pp. 791–798). New York, NY, USA: ACM: (ICML 2007).

[10] Navdeep, J., & Geoffrey, H. (2011). Learning a better representation of speech soundwaves using restricted boltzmann machines. *Speech and Signal Processing (ICASSP) 2011 IEEE International Conference* (pp. 5884–5887). IEEE.

[11] Andre, M., Florent, K., Eric W., T., & Lenka, Z. (2014, Jun 17). Sparse Estimation with the Swept Approximated Message-Passing Algorithm. *Proceedings of the 32nd International Conference on Machine Learning, v1*, pp. 1123-1132.

[12] Kristian, K., Babak, A., & Sriraam, N. (2009). Counting Belief Propagation. *Proceedings of the Twenty-Fifth Conference on Uncertainty in Artificial Intelligence (UAI2009).* Uncertainty in Artificial Intelligence.

[13] Olusegun, O. A., Babatunde, A. N., Omotehinwa, T. O., Aremu, D. R., & Balogun, B. F. (2014, May – June). An Appropriate Search Algorithm for Finding Grid Resources. *International Journal of Emerging Trends & Technology in Computer Science (IJETTCS), 3, Issue 3.*

[14] Todd K, M., & Jacob H, G. (2006). Multiple constraint satisfaction by belief propagation: An example using sudoku. *Adaptive and Learning Systems* (pp. 122 – 126). IEEE Mountain Workshop on 2006.

[15] Scott, K., Ethan, B., & Wheeler, R. (2012). Abstraction-Guided Sampling for Motion Planning. *Proceedings of the Fifth Annual Symposium Combinatorial Search.* Association for the Advancement of Artificial Intelligence (www.aaai.org).

YOUR KNOWLEDGE HAS VALUE

- We will publish your bachelor's and master's thesis, essays and papers

- Your own eBook and book - sold worldwide in all relevant shops

- Earn money with each sale

Upload your text at www.GRIN.com
and publish for free